IT'S TIME TO EAT GREEN PEAS

It's Time to Eat GREEN PEAS

Walter the Educator

Silent King Books
A WhichHead Entertainment Imprint

Copyright © 2024 by Walter the Educator

All rights reserved. No part of this book may be reproduced in any manner whatsoever without written per- mission except in the case of brief quotations embodied in critical articles and reviews.

First Printing, 2024

Disclaimer

This book is a literary work; the story is not about specific persons, locations, situations, and/or circumstances unless mentioned in a historical context. Any resemblance to real persons, locations, situations, and/or circumstances is coincidental. This book is for entertainment and informational purposes only. The author and publisher offer this information without warranties expressed or implied. No matter the grounds, neither the author nor the publisher will be accountable for any losses, injuries, or other damages caused by the reader's use of this book. The use of this book acknowledges an understanding and acceptance of this disclaimer.

It's Time to Eat GREEN PEAS is a collectible early learning book by Walter the Educator suitable for all ages belonging to Walter the Educator's Time to Eat Book Series. Collect more books at WaltertheEducator.com

USE THE EXTRA SPACE TO TAKE NOTES AND DOCUMENT YOUR MEMORIES

GREEN PEAS

It's time to eat, come gather near,

It's Time to Eat

Green
Peas

A bowl of green peas waits right here.

So small and round, a cheerful sight,

A tasty treat in green delight!

Green peas are soft, not hard to chew,

They'll give you strength and vitamins too.

Pop one in, it's fun to munch,

Crunchy, sweet, a perfect lunch!

They grow in pods out in the sun,

Farmers pick them one by one.

Fresh from the garden, so crisp and sweet,

Green peas are such a yummy treat!

Sprinkle them warm on mashed potatoes,

Or mix them up with fresh tomatoes.

Add a bit of butter, just a touch,

Oh, those green peas, you'll love them so much!

It's Time to Eat

Green Peas

Imagine the peas are tiny green balls,

Rolling and bouncing down the hall.

But on your fork, they sit in a line,

Ready to eat, so perfectly fine!

Green peas help you jump and run,

They're full of magic for having fun.

They keep you strong, they help you grow,

Eating your peas will make you glow!

What's that sound? A happy crunch?

Green peas are joining in your lunch!

They cheer you on with every bite,

"Good job!" they say, "You're doing it right!"

Try them plain, or with some cheese,

There are so many ways to eat green peas.

In soups, in pies, or on their own,

It's Time to Eat

Green
Peas

They're the best veggies you've ever known!

So take your fork, don't wait too long,

Sing the green pea-eating song!

"Green peas, green peas, hooray for you!

You're yummy, healthy, and fun to chew!"

Now the peas are gone from your plate,

Your belly feels full, it's feeling great!

Thank you, green peas, for all you do,

It's Time to Eat

Green
Peas

You're the little veggie that makes us new!

ABOUT THE CREATOR

Walter the Educator is one of the pseudonyms for Walter Anderson. Formally educated in Chemistry, Business, and Education, he is an educator, an author, a diverse entrepreneur, and he is the son of a disabled war veteran. "Walter the Educator" shares his time between educating and creating. He holds interests and owns several creative projects that entertain, enlighten, enhance, and educate, hoping to inspire and motivate you. Follow, find new works, and stay up to date with Walter the Educator™ at WaltertheEducator.com

www.ingramcontent.com/pod-product-compliance
Lightning Source LLC
LaVergne TN
LVHW052012060526
838201LV00059B/3995